A Book of Hours

Saint Andrew's Abbey
Valyermo, California

Editor's Note:

Monasticism is intimately involved with time: the time of light moving into darkness, of the passing hours of prayer, of the passing of lives, and of Time itself's ultimate passing. *A Book of Hours*, a book of meditation, using ikonic words and images, illustrates how a contemporary monastery passes, in the monastic day, its present time of pilgrimage; and how that present time is rooted in both personal and communal history, in anticipation of the future. How, despite busyness and, at times, regret and confusion, the monk living his monastic life with diurnal surety, from prayers in the night before dawn, through the seasons of the year, through the slants of light on summer mornings or winter late afternoons, through fire and elusive angels, in hope, and with community, moves towards God.

Aelred Niespolo, O.S.B.

Copyright © 2001 Saint Andrew's Abbey
All rights reserved.
All photos by Phillip Zuckerman, Santa Monica, California, ©
by the photographer. See last page for copyright dates.

PROLOGUE TO THE RULE OF SAINT BENEDICT

We have therefore, to establish a school of the Lord's service. In instituting it we hope to establish nothing harsh or oppressive. But if anything is somewhat strictly laid down, according to the dictates of equity and for the amendment of vices or for the preservation of love; do not therefore flee in dismay from the way of salvation, which cannot be other than narrow at the beginning.

Truly as we advance in this way of life and faith, our hearts open wide, and we run with unspeakable sweetness of love on the path of God's commandments, so that, never departing from his guidance, but persevering in his teaching in the monastery until death, we may by patience participate in the passion of Christ; that we may deserve also to be partakers of his kingdom. Amen.

A short historical notice, Published March 11, 1955

Expelled by the Chinese Communist regime, the monks of St. Benedict's Priory of Chengtu, China, have found a new home in the Archdiocese of Los Angeles. With the authorization of His Eminence James Francis Cardinal McIntyre, Archbishop of Los Angeles, they will soon reopen their monastery under the new name of St. Andrew's Priory on the former Hidden Springs Ranch at Valyermo.

St. Benedict's Priory of Chengtu, founded in 1929 by the famous Abbey of St. Andre, Belgium, conducted a diocesan major seminary and a state-recognized school for non-Catholic students. Shortly after World War II, the Priory established the Institute of Western and Oriental Cultural Studies, with a 10,000 volume library.

On Christmas day, 1949, the Communists took over the city of Chengtu. The Institute was dissolved, the library confiscated, and the Benedictine monks put under house arrest. After three years of hardship, the monks were finally expelled from Communist China in 1952.

In 1954, the parent Abbey of St. Andre in Belgium decided to transfer the Priory to Southern California. The Cardinal-Archbishop of Los Angeles authorized its establishment in the Archdiocese.

Plans for the remodeling of the Hidden Springs Ranch, Valyermo, are ready for execution. A dairy barn will become the monk's living quarters, a stable will be converted to a chapel, where they will celebrate Holy Mass and chant the Divine Office. The main ranch house will be used as a guesthouse for retreatants and visitors who wish to spend a few days of peace and prayer in a monastic atmosphere. Besides leading monastic life and chanting the Divine Office, the monks of St. Andrew's will conduct retreats and devote themselves to intellectual and educational activities. They will also engage in farming, in order to become self-supporting as soon as possible.

The purpose of St. Andrew's Priory in Valyermo is therefore to carry on the ages-old tradition of the Order of St. Benedict, whose motto is – Pray and Work.

Chengtu, China

Hidden Springs Ranch

+Fr. Raphael Vinciarelli, OSB
+Fr. Wilfrid Weitz, OSB
+Fr. Thaddeus Yang, OSB

Youths grow tired and weary,
the young stumble and fall,
but those who hope in Yahweh will regain their strength,
they will sprout wings like eagles,
though they run they will not grow weary,
though they walk they will never tire.
Isiah 40:30-31

Fr. Eleutherius Winance, OSB
+Fr. Vincent Martin, OSB
+Fr. Felix Tang, OSB

+Fr. Alberic Crombrugghe de Loringh, OSB
+Fr. Gaetan Loriers, OSB
Fr. Bernard Hwang
Fr. Werner Papeians de Morchoven, OSB

The First Community
At Valyermo

The monastic vocation is a mystery. Therefore it cannot be completely expressed in a clear succinct formula. It is a gift of God, and we do not understand it as soon as we receive it, for all God's gifts, especially His spiritual gifts share in his own hiddenness and in His own mystery. God will reveal Himself to us in the gift of our vocation, but He will do this only gradually.

We can expect to spend our whole lives as monks entering deeper and deeper into the mystery of our monastic vocation, which is our life hidden with Christ in God. If we are real monks, we are constantly rediscovering what it means to be a monk, and yet we never exhaust the full meaning of our vocation.

Louis Merton, OCSO

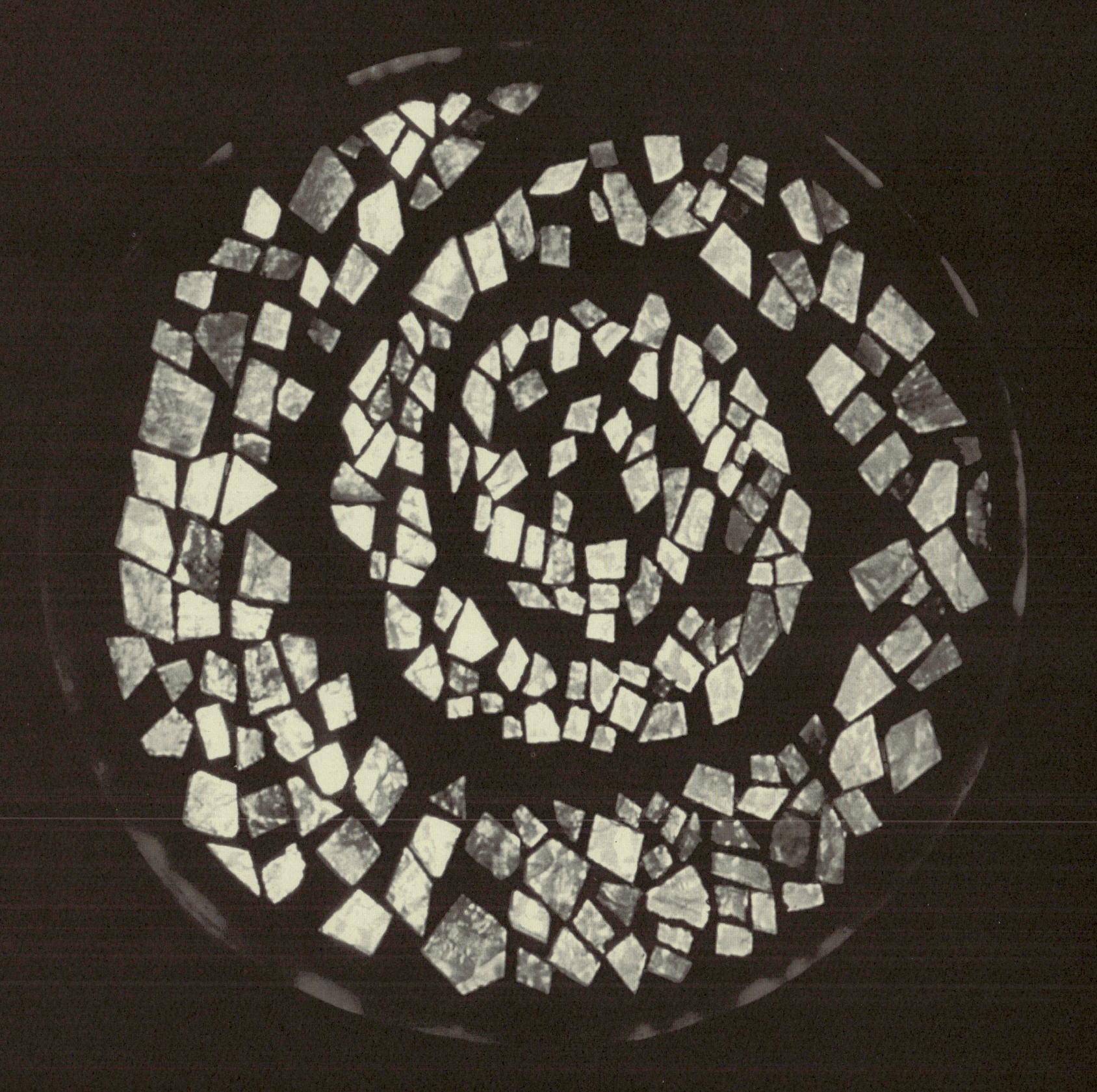

There came to Abba Joseph, Abba Lot, and said to him, 'Father, according to my strength I keep a modest rule of prayer and fasting and meditation and quiet, and according to my strength I purge my imagination: what more must I do?' The old man, rising, held up his hands against the sky, and his fingers became like ten torches of fire, and he said, 'If thou wilt, thou shall be made wholly a flame.'

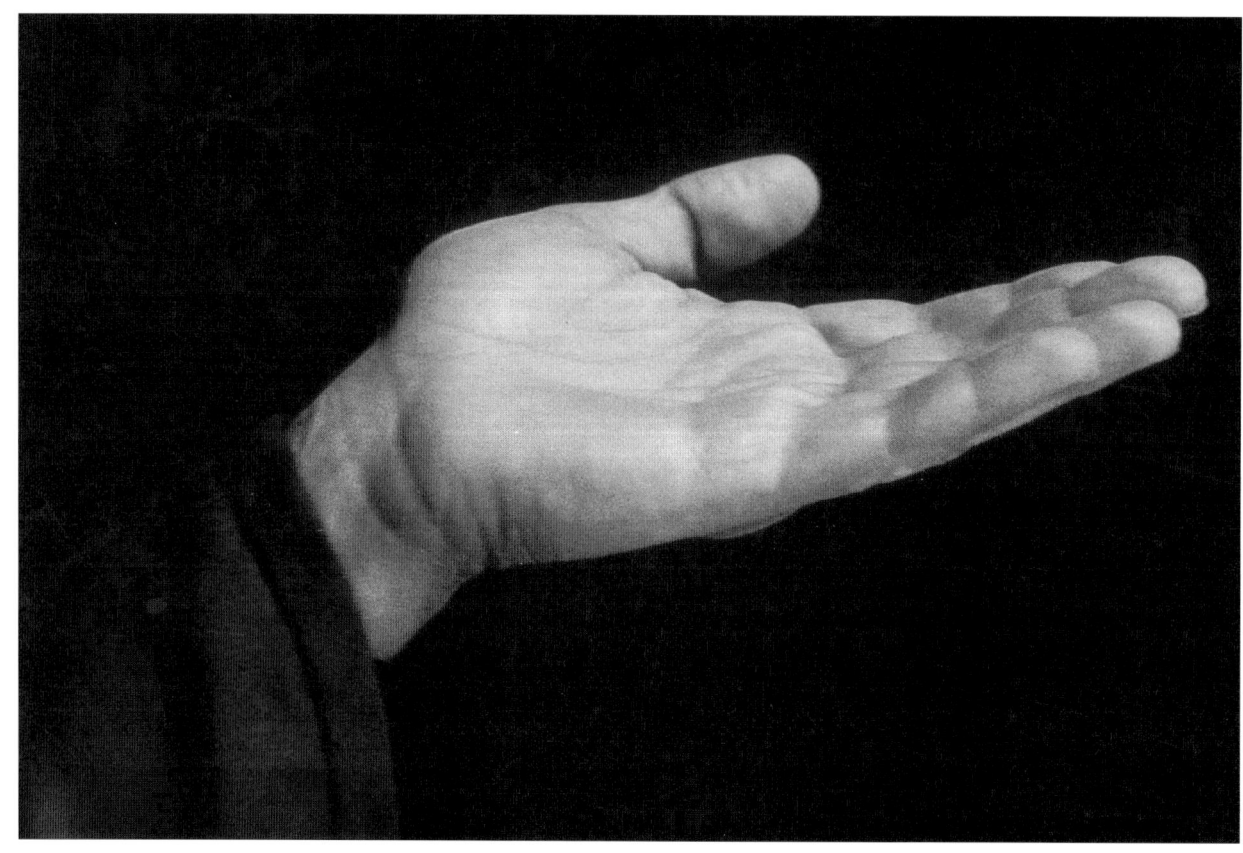

THE ORATORY OF THE MONASTERY

The oratory is to be what it is called, and nothing else should be done or kept there. When the Work of God is finished all should go out in complete silence and with reverence for God, so that a brother who wishes to pray by himself will not be impeded by another's insensitivity. But if he wishes to pray in solitude, he should enter to pray with simplicity, not in a loud voice but with tears and attentiveness of heart. And therefore one who is not performing this work is not to be permitted to remain in the oratory after the Work of God, so that, as was said, no one else is impeded.
Rule of St. Benedict: Chapter 52

VIGILS

Psalm 118

My part, I have resolved, O Lord,
is to obey your word.
With all my heart I implore your favor;
show me the mercy of your promise.
I have pondered over my ways
and returned to your will.
I made haste and did not delay
to obey your commands.
Though the nets of the wicked ensnared me
I remembered your law.
At midnight I will rise and thank you
for your just decrees.
I am a friend of all who revere you,
who obey your precepts.
Lord, your love fills the earth.
Teach me your statutes.

Abba Antony said: 'The man who abides in solitude and is quiet, is delivered from fighting three battles—those of hearing, speech and sight. Then he will have but one battle to fight—the battle of the heart.'

My heart is ready, O God,
my heart is ready.
I will sing, I will sing your praise.
Awake my soul,
awake lyre and harp,
I will awake the dawn.
Psalm 56

LAUDS

Psalm 150

Alleluia!

Praise God in his holy place,
praise him in his mighty heavens.
Praise him for his powerful deeds,
praise his surpassing greatness.

O praise him with sound of trumpet,
praise him with lute and harp.
Praise him with timbrel and dance,
praise him with strings and pipes.

O praise him with resounding cymbals,
praise him with clashing of cymbals.
Let everything that lives and that breathes
give praise to the Lord.

Alleluia!

He shall endure like the sun and the moon
from age to age.
He shall descend like rain on the meadow,
like raindrops on the earth.

In his days justice shall flourish
and peace till the moon fails.
He shall rule from sea to sea,
from the Great River to earth's bounds.
Psalm 71

O that I had wings like a dove
to fly away and be at rest.
So I would escape far away
And take refuge in the desert.
Psalm 54

A brother questioned an old man saying, 'What good work should I do that I may live?' The old man said, 'God alone knows what is good. I have heard it said that one of the Fathers asked Abba Nistheros the Great, the friend of Abba Antony, and said to him, ' What good work is there that I could do?' He said to him, 'Are not all actions equal? Scripture says that Abraham was hospitable and God was with him. David was humble, and God was with him. Elias loved interior peace and God was with him. So, do whatever you see your soul desires according to God and guard your heart.'

DAILY MANUAL LABOR

Idleness is the enemy of the soul; and therefore the brothers should be occupied at certain times in manual labor, and at certain other hours in sacred reading.
Rule of St. Benedict: Chapter 48

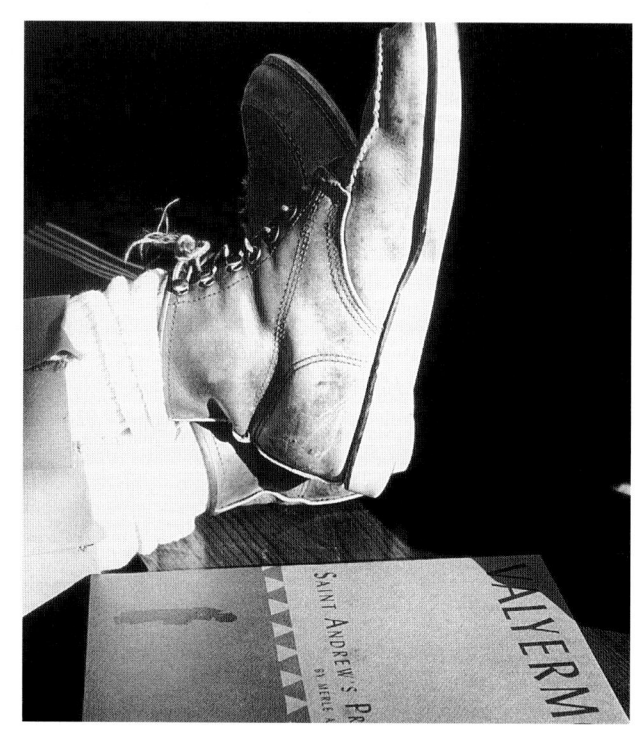

A brother asked Abba Poemen, 'Is it better to speak or to be silent?' The old man said to him, 'The man who speaks for God's sake does well, but he who is silent for God's sake also does well.'

A brother came and stayed with a certain solitary and when he was leaving he said: 'Forgive me, Father, for I have broken in upon your Rule. But the hermit replied, saying: 'My rule is to receive you with hospitality and to let you go in peace.'

THE RECEPTION OF GUESTS

All guests who present themselves are to be received as Christ, for He will say: I was a stranger and you took me in. And to everyone fitting honor is to be shown, especially to those of the household of faith and to pilgrims.
Rule of St. Benedict: Chapter 53

45

EUCHARIST

Psalm 115

I trusted, even when I said:
'I am sorely afflicted,'
and when I said in my alarm:
'no man can be trusted.'

How can I repay the Lord
for his goodness to me?
The cup of salvation I will raise;
I will call on the Lord's name.

My vows to the Lord I will fulfill
before all his people.
O precious in the eyes of the Lord
is the death of his faithful.

Your servant, Lord, your servant am I;
you have loosened my bonds.
A thanksgiving sacrifice I make:
I will call on the Lord's name.

My vows to the Lord I will fulfill
before all his people,
in the courts of the house of the Lord,
in your midst, O Jerusalem.

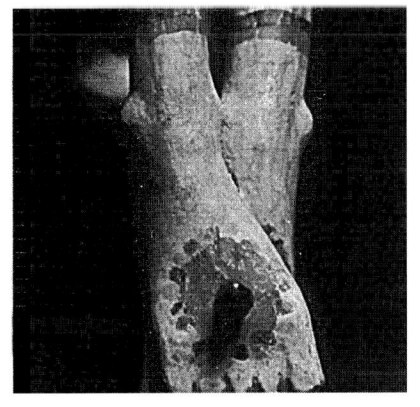

QUALITIES THE ABBOT MUST HAVE

The abbot must always remember what he is, remember what he is called, and know that from him to whom more is committed, more is required. And he must know how difficult and arduous is his received task of ruling souls and serving different temperaments: complimenting some, rebuking others, using persuasion with still others; and according to the unique qualities and intelligence of each he must so conform and adapt himself that not only will the flock committed to him suffer no loss, but he will truly rejoice in the increase of a good flock.
Rule of St. Benedict: Chapter 2

Amma Syncletica said, 'In the beginning there are a great many battles and a good deal of suffering for those who are advancing towards God and afterwards, ineffable joy. It is like those who wish to light a fire, at first they are choked by the smoke and cry, and by this means obtain what they seek (as it is said: "Our God is a consuming fire"): so we also must kindle the divine fire in ourselves through tears and hard work.

THE GOOD ZEAL THAT MONKS OUGHT TO HAVE

Just as there is an evil zeal of bitterness which separates from God and leads to hell, so there is a good zeal which separates from vices and leads to God and to life everlasting. This zeal then, should be practiced by monks with the most fervent love. That is: they should outdo one another in showing honor.

Let them most patiently endure one another's infirmities, whether of body or of character. Let them compete in showing obedience to one another. None should follow what he judges useful for himself, but rather what is better for another:: They should practice fraternal charity with a pure love; to God offering loving reverence, loving their abbot with sincere and humble affection, preferring nothing whatever to Christ, and may be bring us all together to life everlasting. Amen.
Rule of St. Benedict: Chapter 72

A brother questioned an old Man saying, 'What good work should I do that I may live?' The old man said, 'God alone knows what is good. I have heard it said that one of the Fathers asked Abba Nistheros the Great, the friend of Abba Antony, and said to him, "What good work is there that I could do?" He said to him, "Are not all actions equal? Scripture says that Abraham was hospitable and God was with him. David was humble, and God was with him. Elias loved interior peace and God was with him. So, do whatever you see your soul desires according to God and guard your heart."'

VESPERS

Psalm 140

I have called to you, Lord; hasten to help me!
Hear my voice when I cry to you.
Let my prayer arise before you like incense,
the raising of my hands like an evening oblation.

Set, O Lord, a guard over my mouth;
keep watch, O Lord, at the door of my lips!
Do not turn my heart to things that are wrong,
to evil deeds with men who are sinners.

Never allow me to share in their feasting.
If a good man strikes or reproves me it is kindness;
but let the oil of the wicked not anoint my head.
Let my prayer be ever against their malice.

Their princes were thrown down by the side of the rock:
then they understood that my words were kind.
As a millstone is shattered to pieces on the ground,
so their bones were strewn at the mouth of the grave.

To you, Lord God, my eyes are turned:
in you I take refuge; spare my soul!
From the trap they have laid for me keep me safe:
keep me from the snares of those who do evil.

Let the wicked fall into the traps they have set
while I pursue my way unharmed.

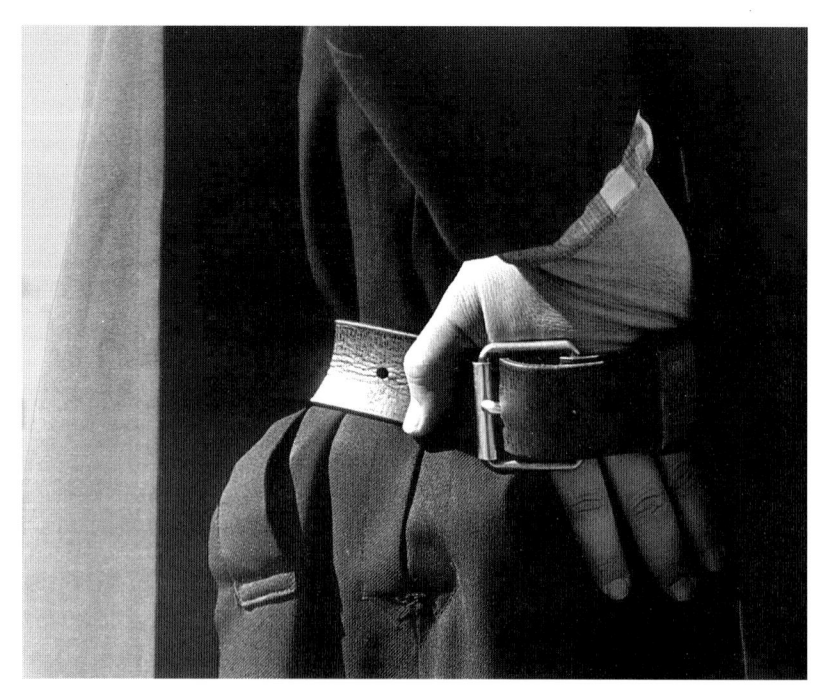

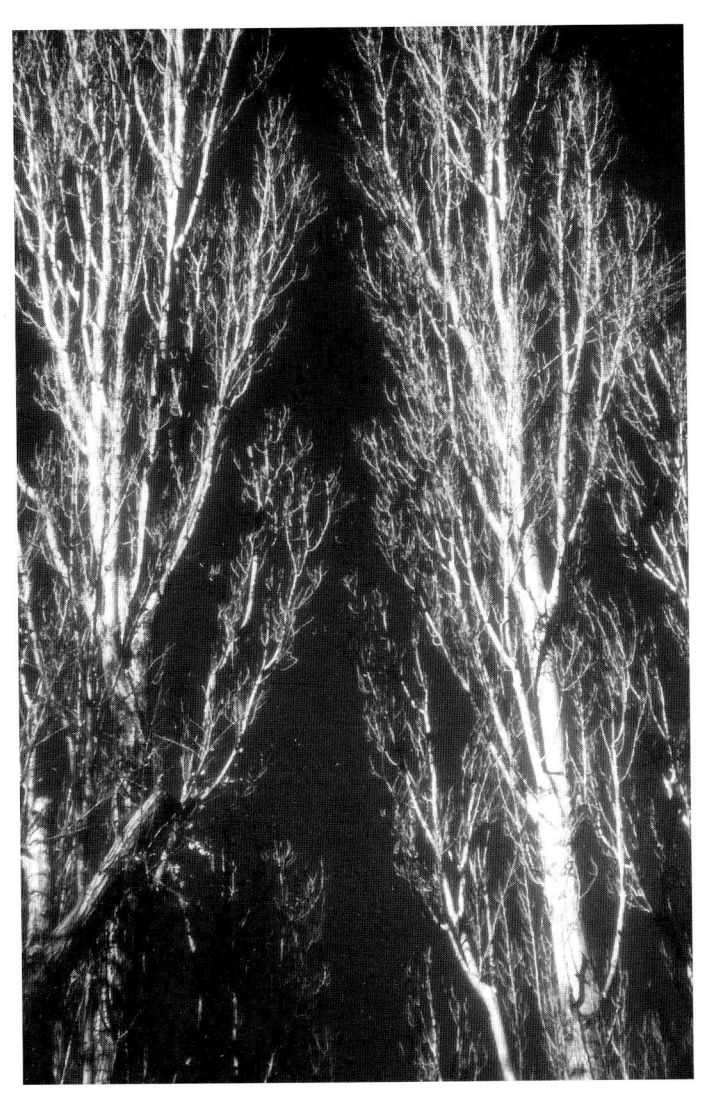

To one of the brethren

appeared a devil, transformed into an angel of light, who said to him:
'I am the Angel Gabriel, and I have been sent to thee.' But the brother said: 'Think again – you must have been sent to somebody else. I haven't done anything to deserve an angel. Immediately the devil ceased to appear.'

Abba Nilus said, 'Do not always be wanting everything to turn out as you think it should, but rather as God pleases, then you will be undisturbed and thankful in your prayers.'

COMPLINE

Psalm 133

O come, bless the Lord,
all you who serve the Lord,
who stand in the house of the Lord,
in the courts of the house of our God.

Lift up your hands to the holy place
and bless the Lord through the night.

May the Lord bless you from Zion,
he who made both heaven and earth.

3 words given: on the Heart

• The Heart is a small vessel, but all things are contained in it: God is there, the angels are there, and there also is life and the kingdom, the heavenly cities and the treasures of grace.

Dimitri of Rostov

• When we are in the Heart, we are at home; when we are not in the Heart, we are homeless.

Theophan the Recluse

• If you have a Heart, you can be saved.

Abba Pambo

Abba Macarius said, 'If we keep remembering the wrongs which men have done us, we destroy the power of the remembrance of God. But if we remind ourselves of the evil deeds of the demons, we shall be invulnerable.'

Abba Sisoes sitting in his cell would ever have his door closed. But it was told of him how in the day of his sleeping, when the Fathers were sitting round him, his face shone like the sun, and he said to them, 'Look, Abba Antony comes.' And after a little while, he said again to them, 'Look, the company of the prophets comes.' And again his face shone brighter, and he said, 'Look, the company of the apostles comes.' And his face shone with a double glory, and lo, he seemed as though he spoke with others. And the old men entreated him, saying, 'With whom are thou speaking, Father?' And he said to them, 'Behold, the angels came to take me, and I asked that I might be left a little while to repent.' The old men said to him 'Thou has no need of repentance, Father.' But he said to them, 'Verily I know not if I have clutched at the very beginning of repentance.'

And they all knew that he was made perfect. And again of a sudden his face was as the sun, and they all were in dread. And he said to them, 'Look, behold the Lord cometh, saying "Bring me my chosen from the desert." And straightway he gave up the ghost. And there came as it might be lightning; and all the place was filled with sweetness.

You sweep men away like a dream,
like grass which springs up in the morning.
In the morning it springs up and flowers:
by evening it withers and fades.
Psalm 89

HUMILITY

Having, therefore ascended all these steps of humility, the monk will soon arrive at that love of God which, being perfect, casts out fear: whereby all that he formerly observed not without dread, he will begin to keep without effort, as if naturally, out of habit; no longer from fear of hell but for the love of Christ, from good habit and delight in virtue. This God through the Holy Spirit will now grant his laborer to manifest, cleansed from vices and sins.
Rule of St. Benedict: Chapter 7

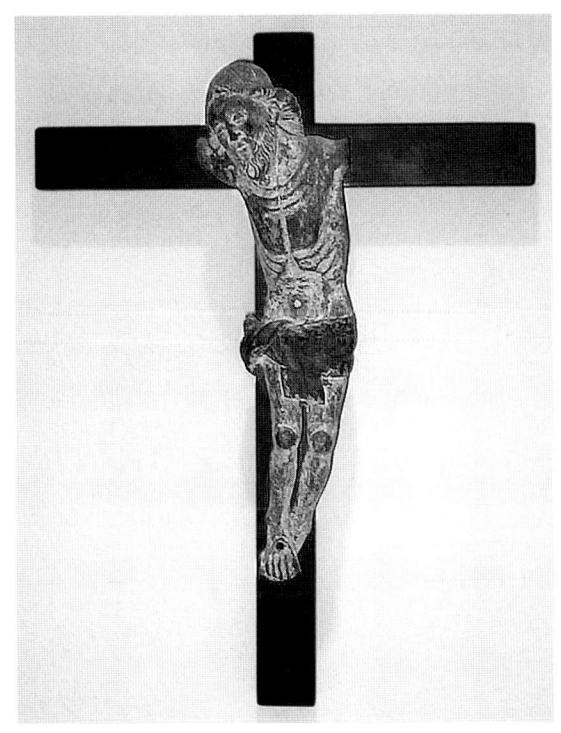

'I am far removed from your sight'
I said in my alarm.
Yet you heard the voice of my plea
when I called for help.
Psalm 30

Τί τοῦτο;
σήμερον σιγὴ
πολλὴ ἐν τῇ γῇ·
Something strange is happening – there is a great silence on earth today, a great silence and stillness.
The whole earth keeps silence because the **K**ing is asleep. The earth trembled and is still because **G**od has fallen asleep in the flesh and he has raised up all who have slept ever since the world began. **G**od has died in the flesh and hell trembles with fear. I order you, O sleeper, to awake. I did not create you to be held a prisoner in hell. **A**rise from the dead for I am the life of the dead. **A**rise, work of my hands, **A**rise, O my likeness: you who were created in my image.
Ἀνάστα ἐκ τῶν νεκρῶν·
Ἐγώ εἰμι η ζωὴ τῶν νεκρῶν.

Photographic notes

Many of the photographs in this book are archival and are without attribution. All other photographs are copyrighted under the photographer's name. The editor thanks Phillip Zuckerman for the fine series of monastic photographs taken specifically for A Book of Hours. Several examples of his earlier work are included. In the case of non-attributed photographs Saint Andrew's Abbey requires written permission to reprint. In the case of all attributed photographs, written permission must be obtained from the photographer.

Attributed Photographs

Cover:
"St. Benedict" © 2001 by Phillip Zuckerman.
Batik designed by Monica Hannash.

Vigils:
"Spiral Stained Glass" © 2001 by Phillip Zuckerman.
Window made by Fairbanks, Fairbanks.
Pg. 10 "Upturned hand" © by Craig Boder.
Pg. 11 "Vigil light" © by Toni Flynn.
Pg. 14 "Leaf fall" © Rosenys.
Pg. 19 "Monk and Window"(diptych), © 2001 by Phillip Zuckerman.
Pg. 21 "Crucifixion" © by Michael Warwick.
Steel sculpture created by Leo Fecht.
Pg. 23 "Joebird", worldwide photos © Damian Dovarganes.

Lauds:
Pg. 25 "Harp" © Brian Lanker.
Pg. 30 "The Prophet Elijah" © 2001 by Phillip Zuckerman.
Pg. 31 "Chapel: side view and doorway" © 1985 by Phillip Zuckerman.
Pg. 32 "Light and Shadow" © 2001 by Phillip Zuckerman.
Pg. 33 "Crucifix" © 2001 by Phillip Zuckerman.
Crucifix by Steven Berardi.
Pg. 34 "Book", Los Angeles Times Photo, © David Bohrer.
Pg. 35 "Fr. Werner" © 2001 by Phillip Zuckerman.
Pg. 36 "Kitchen" © 2001 by Phillip Zuckerman.
Pg. 37 "Kitchen Work" (diptych) © 2001 by Phillip Zuckerman.
Pg. 38 "Breakfast Talk" © 2001 by Phillip Zuckerman.
Pg. 38 "Shoes" © Caroline Luckhardt.
Pg. 39 "Field Work" © 2001 by Phillip Zuckerman.
Pg. 41 "Breakfast", Los Angeles Times Photo, © David Bohrer.
Pg. 45 "Ducks" © Thomas Frenn.
Pg. 46 "Festival" © Rosenys.
Pg. 48 "Crowds" © Sean McClory.
Pg. 49 "Walk Away" © Caroline Luckhardt.

Eucharist:
"Crucifix" © 2001 by John Lewis.
Crucifix carved by Jose Benito Ortega.
Pg. 51 "Three Views" © 2001 by John Lewis.
Pg. 53 "Monastic Albs" © 1984 by Phillip Zuckerman.
Pg. 54 "Monk vesting" Los Angeles Times Photo, © David Bohrer.
Pg. 55 "Profession", Los Angeles Times Photo, © David Bohrer.
Pg. 56 "Monks in Chapel I" (diptych) © 2001 by Phillip Zuckerman.
Pg. 58 "Oblation" © 2001 by Phillip Zuckerman.
Pg. 59 "Chalices and Hosts" © 1984 by Phillip Zuckerman.
Pg. 60 "Monks Singing" © 2001 by Phillip Zuckerman.
Pg. 61 "Monks in Chapel II" © 2001 by Phillip Zuckerman.

Vespers:
Pg. 68 "Belt" © by Caroline Luckhardt
Pg. 70 "Choir Monks", Los Angeles Time Photo, © David Bohrer.
Pg.72 "Luke" Los Angeles Times Photo, © David Bohrer.
Pg. 73 "St. Andrew" © 2001 by Phillip Zuckerman.
Batik designed by Monica Hannash.
Pg. 75 "Winter Scene" © by Suzanne Farley.

Compline:
Pg 89 "The Annunciation" © 2001 by Phillip Zuckerman.
Pg. 91 "Benediction" © 2001 by Phillip Zuckerman.
Pg. 93. "Moon" © Chris Rapp.
Back Cover: logo designed by Laurent Chapman, OSB

The editor is grateful to Fr. Werner Papiens de Morchoven, OSB for opening up to him the many riches of the St. Andrew's Abbey archives. He thanks Fr. Paul Pluth, OSB for his graphics (and graphic) advice, Fr. Luke Dysinger OSB for his technical assistance. Thanks also to Source Books, California, distributors of Fr. Dysinger's edition of the Rule of St. Benedict. He is most grateful to Richard Rice and the staff at The Candlelight Press for their generosity, kindness and enthusiasm.
Copyright © 2001 Saint Andrew's Abbey

Nihil amore Christi praeponere.

To prefer nothing to the love of Christ.